HAIL

MATTHEW ROTANDO

POEMS

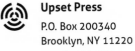

Upset Press
P.O. Box 200340
Brooklyn, NY 11220
upsetpress.org

Established in 2000, UpSet Press is an independent press based in Brooklyn. The original impetus of the press was to upset the status quo through literature. UpSet Press has expanded its mission to promote new work by new authors; the first works, or complete works, of established authors—placing a special emphasis on restoring to print new editions of exceptional texts; and first-time translations of works into English. Overall, UpSet Press endeavors to advance authors' innovative visions, and works that engender new directions in literature.

Cover art by Arturo Elizondo: "Young Kafka, a Dalai Lama"
Book design by Wendy Lee / wendyleedesign.com

Library of Congress Control Number: 2016957904
ISBN 9781937357887
Printed in the United States of America

For Dolores and Axel, and always for Todd

i.

...all ashes, all ashes again.

—*from "On Neal's Ashes," by Allen Ginsberg*

A Peculiar Caravan

The tiny letters that make words also travel through windshields, through your eyes, across tables, and past mausoleum doors. Some of these letters have attained a strange resonance. Inside the e's, skeleton heads wobble and clack, their garnet teeth glinting in the weary glow of your little nightlight. Someone has dropped an old green jacket on the k's. They have fallen again, into their sleep of uselessness. Also, the b's and t's are wrapped in a wild embrace. They are crying and won't let go of each other. You walk around all day in clothes, tiring the world. Every night, the tree outside your window has a nightmare about a campfire. In winter, as you ready yourself for bed, it scratches strange new letters onto the frosted glass. You dream new words with them, outlandish shapes the world has yet to see. By morning they have all trundled off in a strange caravan. But they remember how you laughed, your arms open wide, while you chased them.

The Very Winters

Your ocean's broken at the shore, at oxygen, at the club for dancing yourself into the floor. The downed flower was the way you knew the case was over. There was everything everywhere and you switched hats until you warmed the very winters within. Usually you'll have the usual. It's expected. Debt is the prick of reality's vapor, makes you know that number's real. And debt burns you down, too. You feel and age, an old whiskey feeling. You work so you don't have to try so hard, but things—all of them—get all the way in the way.

Traveling Outside

Truth is eight times old,
And this car goes three minutes per hour.
I can't write a poem called "Man Alone."
Bright city lights won't let me,
And my craft is headed back to earth.
My shields are deeper within
Than they are wide
On the outside.
I'm widening my search,
And I haven't found anything of which
A time traveler wouldn't approve.
So I go back to the past
And wear my best clothes.
Shifts in space
Make my corpse full of surprises.
I step into it
And make everything happen.

On Memory

I have just woken from a dream in which I ran into my dear friend, S., after many years. In the heat of the afternoon, at the same moment, we each turned a dusty corner on a quiet street of our old town, which I happened to be visiting. To my pleasure and surprise, there was S., thin and loping, and wishing me a good day. I embraced him of a sudden, and he took several confused steps backward. He did not remember me. I could hardly believe it. We had not seen each other for some years, but we had shared so much. We once walked and laughed together, many miles, in the blistering desert. We had browsed the cramped markets together in the Valley of the Brave. We used to spend hours in silent meditation, sitting alongside each other and breathing. I tried to remind him of his love for huitlacoche and for the chocolate sapote, and for the wings of men. He shook his head in silence. I recalled how we once appeared to each other in the hills, summoning one another with our thoughts. Bewildered, S. remembered nothing. I recounted in detail how we laughed at the wind when it dislodged and flung poorly attached shingles from the roof of the little mountain house we once lived in. I reminded him of how he comforted me after I had to leave a woman I loved, who had been his friend. He stared into the distance. I told him of one of his own lovers laughing and throwing her head back and tossing firecrackers from windows of moving cars. I told him of how he taught me to be patient, very patient, when sautéing mushrooms, and to use more butter than I thought appropriate. None of it came back to his mind. He could not even recall my face. I began to wonder if I had invented him. He certainly looked like the S. I thought I knew, but since he neither remembered me, nor our experiences together, was it not feasible that I had created him, that I had made his likeness a character for my own use? Was it possible that I had never been to The Brave Valley, had never savored the huitlacoche, and, indeed, had only dreamed myself into such scenes, using the template of S.'s face as a companion in my imagining? Perhaps I was a mirrored reflection of the forgetfulness of S. Perhaps my memories, which I had cherished so hotly, were pure invention, immaterial as wishes. I tore at my chest with my hands, and trudged from the street where we met. I looked back only once and saw him, perplexed, holding my black wings in his arms. They had fallen into the dust when I turned away.

A Story Told And A Sketch Of Vincent Price And A Laugh From A Horse's Mouth, Doing A Bit

Daddy issues for everybody. Plenty of room for histrionics. Everyone was doing a stand-up job, but blowing the punchline. Even though you said your name, I still forgot your character. It was a disconnect, and it's personally insulting, despite the leather effigy and Mick Jagger's ability to do it right and be a scary good soldier. The scene cut is this: two minutes before we grasp this moment, we find ourselves on skis, not even paying attention, but feeling like a million bucks. I love that feeling, like an athlete, without caring about approval. Who tells someone they are overtalking? People will strive to seek approval of someone who does the firing in person. Everything is sideways and you take it personally. The gnome calls you about all the reasons why, finally, and you want it to be true. But it's your imagination giving you the advice. Your performance watches you and says dollars are not really anything; very Buddhalike. At the end of the day it's you approving you, and the cliché of it clashes with the neuroses of the host, alongside the history of personalities. And I know you're acting the part, but when you find yourself doing it, it could be misinterpreted as weird, because of your family history of insanity. People who stayed the longest stayed because they felt like they belonged. Is the astronaut joke a joke, or just a reality? What was he looking for when he worked the probe, while he looked in my eyes, with his perfect afro? There was a ready symmetry to things. Like we'd made it to the waiting room during a long walk. Shiny, efficient, like we were going to win.

Ethics

The horror of time was that beauty made us pull our-
selves together, close our eyes and whisk stuff around
in the kitchen. The things we said we'd say we said.
Then we predicted what came next. The good things
fell apart and you became an agent, investigating your
illness. You pulled me under and I covered my eyes
with my history of other loves. Here's to Saint Hon-
esty, sack of grief. This is the worst. It's not even a
thing. It's just what I get for trying to ride the dog.
There's some shame in saying I love what I love. Not
enough to keep me from saying it.

Them Just Goes

We're not about giving up or giving away the mental. We're about correcting for echoes. We're about gathering details and the smoky bottom. We're about trash; like all the waters, we refuse to go down hoses...but we go. Them is a way to start; them raspy details. Deets. Hangtags wimpling in the storeshadows of a frantic year. The fervent all-out sureness makes us seem ugly to the bodies that grew up around us. We, in our bodies, in our aches and skin, in our swilling holes full of robbers and liars. We laugh and cry, return and pick some how-to chatter. Them is not a way to go, them just goes. The phone you were on was a stalling effect for doing what you do. If you touch only sheer things, you'll touch elusive fingers under your smoking ghost hands. Smoke, it really has a hold on your imagination. This is a problem, as your imagination is not an organ. Not a skinnable thing, just a skinning echo.

Animals And Instruments

Without hard work the sad man gets nowhere. He needs music and now there is silence. The sad man buys food and watches movies and eats and has the worst dream in the world. He wakes up troubled because he dreamed he was trying to lock the doors and could not. He could not lock the doors and everyone kept coming in while he tried to work and think. They tried to name him Hugh, and Stan, and Hank. All these hefty, big-handed names. But he simply wanted them to leave or be quiet while he sat at his bench in the basement making tricky things from wood. Animals and little houses and musical instruments out of little chunks of mahogany and pine that he would carve intricately and slowly when he could keep the people that called him Hank from always calling him Stan and always opening his door and talking to him. Soon he would move to a quiet part of town, where no one knew his name and he would pretend to be impossible, or imaginary. There, people would give him unapproachable names like Victor, or Dennis. They would leave him alone. And he would make better animals and instruments there, by far, with much quieter hands.

A Cork In The Floor Comes Out

Chaos can't tangle. Only carcomido can. Only trash and ruddy hands can tango. Only tragicomic grunions running under math can burden or can share. Only rusted bodies and boding clouds can rut in angled canyons. Chaos can rankle, but can't drone. Candles can drone in a visual way, though if a badness, they cannot. Tarnation cancels codes, cancels orders, cancels every swing. Yesterday can take root, leave a mark, and turn. It does so every day. If feet have their way, the worker goes away. The wording holds and tangents tersely fix the mode of going. Each caustic breach of trust camps within encomiums. And mottled hills are grey. And green chili, red chili, hair in my mouth, all of it goes wondering through a fever, through a span of night, a brace of rain. Some wired wisdom talker rides a bike through fields; we are there, we are there, we write shields with our mouths. I lend you a towel, you dry. After the thing, there's its -ness. We speak in close silences, and tangle. So yes can tangle. It can, and chaos, too.

My Closet

When I was seven years old I moved into a new house with my dad, his new bride, and her daughter. I had a big room and a big walk-in closet. I was amazed at how much space I had all to myself. Thrilling. Some little kids might think a big dark closet was a creepy place. Not me. I would turn the lights off in my room and go into the closet and turn the lights out in there too. Utter blackness amazed me. My mind went wild with vivid thoughts and waking dreams. I would wrap a pillow around my head so I could see and hear completely nothing. I wanted "imperceptible air."

In my complete quiet dark, I would sit on the floor and try and intensely will myself to see. See what? See seeing. I know I am giving my adult language to something I didn't have words for at seven years old. But in the absence of the senses I would try to see seeing and hear hearing. There would be the initial afterglow in the retinas from turning out the lights, but then that would burn away and I would be there in an ocean of black. And my ears, at first, seemed occupied with trying to be sure of silence and would hear their own suggestion of sounds. But then those would fade and I would be just this perceiving thing, this -ness, without any perceptions. I loved it.

I remember it so vividly and fondly. Fondly, I think, because even though I started this activity at seven, I kept doing it, again and again, until I moved out of the house to go to college. Me, crouching on the floor in a sense-deprived vessel of my own crude design. I would hover in this nothing-womb and then go a step further. Once I had eliminated my most active senses, I was aware of nothing but thought. I had shut down my mind's need to attend to anything but conceiving of things. I would imagine myself huddled there in the closet, then I would push even my imagination into the nothing. It was like trying to get to the perfect void. But then I would hit this fulfilling paradox...which is where, once I touched it, I was always trying to get back to and simply "hang out" in: if I could fully conceive of the complete void, of a perfect absence of myself, then there was still some kind of mind, or me, there doing the conceiving.

So, I thought, as an analog to the above paradox, death is either the completion of this effort to be the ultimate peace of the total void, a quiet fulfillment of not-me; or, in death, there was still some kind of mind capable of conceiving of itself, thus making death not an annihilation but a transition to a bodiless state of perception. And whatever physical or emotional pains accompanied dying were just the burning away of the senses, which I was used to. Doing this over and over in my youth, I was perhaps trying to touch the very thin curtains that made up the fabric and the idea of the soul, and then part them and walk through.

Lost Cities

This despicable knot, hated man, unkind to doors. I have him in my eye, as a sir, and as a daring bird. He remembers not. I am the one who remembers, alone in his dead house. His roots slip out and dissolve. He topples and lands, again and again, as the ghost of a different metropole. Pompeii, Mohenjo-daro, Tikal.

I Haven't Been Comfortable Enough To Take Anyone For Granted In Years

Just McCorkel. Old Rusty McCheswick. Eye stand, deer stand, shadow. You happier, you buy and wide. You stalk a grey tree. But I'm glad, because you're Canadian, and my boyfriend wears your shirts. He never mixed with my parents, or really even tried. Coney Island had to do. You can, you know, Canadian. You mix parts of your life, can you bring parrots? Have you met who we just hired, the participles? There's farming and using an axe. Do you have a problem with chicken? The yams. The two ways we should work together, the pants, the dysfunction of this. The lesson I take from this is that a guy like your dad *is* what he does. On TV, even when they kick you out, they don't really mean it. I *love* that.

Why My Breakfast Calls Me Billy
I Don't Know

We're not ignoring Big Billy Chuckface anymore. He's so overjoyed and free of regret we just don't feel we have to fuck with him. He's towering over a pier, knocking it down with the edge of his hand. He's got amnesia. He loves us. He loves us still. Drunken, we hit him with a hammer while he slept and he didn't see any tragedy in that. His fortune is pure, liberated from worry about art and production. His death is not fearful to him. He is sixty feet tall. He is about welcoming, about feeling like a savior, illogical, shining a gift-giving light on kids and oldies. His face beams. Old Billy. Old and sweet and packed with gala events, we bow to him. We are the eggs. We are the cornbread. We rode all the rides at the Abuse Park and unchuckable Billy nurtured us, salved our blisters and bruises. Flies gather at the corners of our eyes and he knocks them away, harmoniously, without anger. He is the Jim-Dandy Crisis, the apotheosis of image. An apocalypse of voice, his Omega pops our dogma boil. We met him in the city. He took us to his country of unloathing. Next to him, in him, we become an us, an I. He makes us feel capital, just tops. Bueno. Biggo. Guillermo. Guillaume. He's taking us into his food tube. We become His stuff.

An Old Electricity

I am an instance of the effect, the cataract of fire and the midnight of time. I go rummaging today, via and voilà, an intruder in snow shadow. I contain accents, establish verbs, and drive forward into a ditch without submitting. Seriously, we should talk about anything at all.

All the paying customers are abed. Some long dead emperor counts the shadows that move beneath his high dome, tosses down leaves, alarms his subjects. Last night I sensed an old electricity, said so, and sent out warmth from my hands. My last entreaty will be silent.

Once met, well met. Eerie hello-women peer at us through wet sheets. Distant dogs and distant trains. A cork in the floor comes loose.

To make is to be. In this manner, an artist knows storm essence.

Three Questions

What if there was a way to tear everything everywhere in half? I can see superlatives shorn, and even the blue Pacific. The signs show and thighs are simple essays to smith on chocks of stone. I tap my fist in sundry dreams and land rolls away. All the shadows we go for, we use to rupture ourselves. I turn out to be monolithic man, born for the beginning. This is the fresh relegation of words you shack with, the many people we show our underclothes. To find rhythm is to gain evidence against slaughter and to initiate slaughter. I can see us cheer in the black dark, the box we grew into. That was not a way to end anything. I listen to the wall crack against my hand while I enact the force of waiting. Elsewheres are the habits we catalog when we touch what we don't want. It's only a problem when we do things. I feel the crud of all these we's and you's in the short term. Can I abandon the whorl of ago? What if time was just a way to chill? The cold people are in me and they dance when I see shards of ice falling off trees.

In Homelike Need

In grungy cross-boats, everything changes and every-
one ruts. The hills on the shoulders of men and ladies
go daring. Their chasms collide in spoken baffles and
boots. Like ten times ago you cleared your throat and
shook a tree to see if people would grow away from
their skins. Like switching to a new childhood that
didn't have a swingset or a shard of wild glass. Liv-
er and runts togethering in your window and pan, so
wicker and shake to the sound of the old man has had
his fun; so whisper and shake to the day the old man
can't dance; so wisdom and steak for dinner or some
such baloney. That washes away the hurting or the
frame of mind that made the sting go feeble, shook
the stench from fingers.

In dream, he held a sharpened sword and showed his
friends how to cut paper squares that floated on air.
All was well, or at least possible, and the edge was
sharp indeed. In homelike need I'll find myself and
my tan brain or my fishy upbringing will trigger a way
to the smashing top of all this. Yes, someone said
smashing, the verb of the day, accept it as adjective,
too. She asks how the day goes, she says how the
waves are full today, she is Lady Liberty and we've
decided to bring her down this night, but instead we'll

get mints. The double cigarette technique produces continuous non-recognition. So it could make you horny. That was my somethingth declaration, I'm too terribly bored to go back and count. Plus, I was a graffiti smear on your highway bathroom.

Then the children we were came out to see the adults we became and a breadlike thing did a painful dance in the oven, once it got old. The heat worked, we were always warm, and the floors were smooth enough to slide on. Even the dog slipped sometimes. You could play music and run circles around the living room and the dog would slip and yip after you. So you did that. It created a message and story about dogs to tell the future. See? The hands I'm wearing, warming me from the basement. Shake and run and feel the thrill of the approaching boogeyman. Now I have star stickers in my wallet and can feel the worth of them, in the dark.

Sort Of A _____ Craquelure

Magnetism by fire. Seams chewed free from the afternoon. Skyscrapers. Long nights with a great friend.

Light steams out my old window face, clears the crucible city and runs home in a rush. Some sonic landscape. A declination of magic makes its own magic. They (those ones with arms and loss) ripple a whole beach, redo spasms of new memory, travel further in. Glinting metal everywhere, surprise meat shudders away, plays the uncomfortable witness.

We made machines. Then machines made time for us. Substantial as knuckles or will. But the city is a device of time, home to all the souls that ever were—catch them in photographs, a headstone, that mossy old tenement brick. All those nouns squirting reticules of memory.

Who is the sheriff of time: fundament or frangible thing? Pauses, expectation of an event. We got caught peering out of a loophole in luck's curtain. Something crenelated, something drawn. Stand next to words, fake or freak meaning, hamper every permanence.

Shin guard, chin guard. We look away, but always bend back to original seeing.

Clouds and Flood

Spend all energy on what you fear, you broken rapturous fleeting thing. You try to bestow meaning and the pram falls over. The baby you spent months and years on turns into a plume of colors and goes away. For good? You don't know and can't. Every broken thing is born. Your eyes are knees. You fall on them when awe takes you away to a sea of wonder, of regret, the seas of so many thinks. Clouds in your vision are slowly spinning stones, they geode open like books as rainglass falls in your drinking cup. You try to ride away, but your hands make mud as you crawl in your bed. You thought it was the road. Here is the page that makes woe something physical to get around, into something unafraid. Is woe afraid of you? You look to the soil, to the box you'll be burned in, to the spare decorations on the pine planks, tiny burnmarks and birdfeet. Inside, unseeable, are symbols made by a carpenter's hammer, hard to make out in the zero light of ground. You will not end in the ground, but as ashes on the sea, drifting down from mountains, reassembling a world from nowhere. A dog squeals. No one speaks. These meditations, these retried phrases. You retire them as soon as they make it to the world. This broken ball's paper pocket. Then a vast suchness, a knowing of numbers, brimming in reedy retinas, all gone and full of open phrases. Brackish arms come up from bogs, pale and grasping for your face. Transparent, you glimpse them before you are borne into the flood.

The Cradle

Shaking hands. Busted tablature. Fiddle sounds and a rejected swimmer. Tingling sun moments and a bright beach pail from your earliest memory.

Cue the piano, line up at every restaurant that wants you. That's all of them? But your green dress, that easy smile. I fell so easily.

I whisper so loudly now, through tears, about what we once held. We were a cradle, you must sense that, that nurtured everything we wished we could actually say.

The Whale

Candles and wine and pasta for kindling. Some pusher whispers the hype in your ear and you appreciate the cards the first time. The whale takes the road and not the sea. The turnout was pretty intense at the last fight between parents. Everyone waited in their seats to see the end and the battle was sooo tragic and yet victorious. We have to be something more than what we expect of ourselves with so many damned mistakes winning us back. Something like that, you know? Yeah. Something like that. You have to do different things, when you eat all the beef you've been eating. Like you have to be prepared not to come down all the way, you have to stay up, you don't know what might happen mentally, you have to keep the engine running. You have to mimic someone who's not tired or dejected at all.

Invitation

What: Some long-suffering thing about ways, or the front's ability to challenge all of time's harbors. Where: Beside a desert of forgotten collectibles. When: Sixteen if you're lucky, but probably more like thirteen, when you started realizing you had reason (the pretty luggage of a mind) that brought more chaos to the halls than most kids around you could even conceive.

Temple Temple, Walls And Doors

I am dank angel, ready wine, the anti-cure. An instance of guitar dropped on the desert. I am a rare crease in time. These hands, my fleeting fists, this continent. I have walked to the edge. This rusting freedom. Near the black door I hang my head, my father's gun against the wall. These nails, this pre-grace, this balkanized love. I feel only wind, and my ragged chest. My gaze and my jar brim with eyes and fingers. My apples, my boy fears, my sliding face and mouth, my quiet. I have no patience, no measure. I cannot open a tiny window.

My jaw is the witch of wasted stories. I am western suns and the hot mouth of dreams. We loved for thirty thousand years, until we were only beetle shells and sand.

Mucho.

The occasion is closed. The dog is closed. The dark is closed. Problem? Closed. Political cartography is closed. Clams is closed. Gates is closed. Closed the storm windows of Oklahoma. Closed the cellar. Mysterious underwater cavern closed. Marsh spirits closed. Closed quick. Closed slow. Closed the election, the gluon, the quark. Closed the collision. The adhesion. Closed the insertion of forethought, family planning, and government. Highlights is closed. Trampolines. Halloween. The harvest moon. The General Store is closed. Stories. Celebrity appearances. Cerrado. Muy cerrado. Chairs is closed. Ruins is closed. Handpainting, rushes to judgment and fake beards is all closed. Nobody is closed. Even mind is closed. Faraway and close is closed. Brother and uncle and phone calls is closed. Rum and milk and tomato is closed. Good is closed. And malo. The uppercut is closed. Closed is the backfist and the drumbeat of war. Closed the whore and the outcast, the coyote, the shofar. Closed the long walk to the cross. Closed the dung beetle, closed the id. And snakes is closed. Nada. The pool. The dojo and the yogin. Burnt offerings closed. Buffaloes and earthworms and the compass. All directions closed. The sign is closed. Closed the sun, and the summation. And the the.

And Again You

And again You: face for a gathering. A YOU face...*a-you-FACE!* (Italian accent), my doll, *my Matt Doll!* (my mom's accent). Oh you held me and I wanted to stay.

In the classrooms they are chanting vowels. Who's chanting? A lesson. Chant now: "Where are you going, Big Pig? *To dig. I'm going to Dig.* And What will you dig, Big Pig? *A bit white turnip.*" This and the vowels as they unfold, or unfetter, or calcify in soup or a name for a place, or a shaming place.

Your face hears its name and brightens, collects, re-draws old storybooks, maps to the treasure in the yard, the hidden coins, the snakeskin, cigar box with some of your baby teeth, a tonic against memory loss. But it goes, you watch it. Muhammad Ali, his hands shake now almost uncontrollably, says

"I was twenty...twenty what? Twenty-two. Now I'm fifty-four. Fifty-four." He said nothing for a minute or so. Then he said, "Time flies. Flies. Flies. It flies away." Then, very slowly, Ali lifted his hand and fluttered his fingers like the wings of a bird.*

*Last paragraph from David Remnick's *King of the World: Muhammed Ali and the Rise of An American Hero* (xvii).

Weird Gravel

Vanity makes its own hole. I am the tip of an honorary spear. Then forgive me. Forgive me again for my thoughts. My homegrown cadence of betrayal and confession. All of imagination. Then the newness of a bruised love, recovering. Then tragedy of sex. Then octopus of orgasm and pleasure of you slapping my face. Wearing sheets at breakfast. Syrup and tears. Too many if only too many to think. Someone has to watch your back, even if it's me.

Beating Due Headfakes

A window or an asp will show you where you took your wrong turn. Neptune has certain objects that we possess, as fellows of the universe, but now is not the time to claim them. Nor is it the time to let Neptune know we are cohabitants. In time, in time. Hands agree to write as we get smarter, even as the knots of knowing fall away. This is the age of tessellated thought. Images bounce back at us for a grand undoing. Alone or along the window, our serpentine mental actions come back around. Time is the culprit, even as it is merely an invented thing. Yesterday, or the future, only exist in thought, and thinking only happens in the present. Therefore the present is the only thing. Don't think of it as a gift. It simply is. If something simply is, and you know it, don't clap your hands.

The Bath Of Time

Everyone I know who says you can't go back to the past lives there. The sun is 865,000 miles in diameter. That means almost nothing, next to the depth of time. Your skin is flying off at just about the same speed that it grows back, until a little man with a bushy black mustache sneaks in your window, chuckles, and puts you to sleep. He takes off his hat and gloves before he goes to work. Goats bleat in the distance. No one feels the room go cold. No one listens for the snakes in the carpet. The blood in your throat tastes like rust. You wave and weakly wave goodbye goodbye. The soft skin on your hand moves through the air like an arc of water tossed from a bucket.

Staying

Tickling the ticking world, the giggling girl. The freak resonance of sequins in your hollow fists, the sheer butter of the pavement you feel when going fast. The trance of the past. Continuance of night deliberations. All and more, and more. Once you saw me enter and my talk dropped off, I was something beyond a telephone, and we bodied. It was effective and there was a slight intermission. Shady telegrams from the future quit arriving. The intelligence of cities and plays was all full of music. Even the movements of our hands overlaid us with pauses. We were some kind of void that time could fill. Then dim pillars buckled and hands opened on wings and someone's loved one passed away, then another, and another. We held the beats within us. The wonder of the future is a crash of waiting and staying cold. Some knowing is too much. That's the brink we walk away from. How walking wakes our wonder, we may know.

What Of Action, Of December

It's warm and our lights are out. The torch song un-
spools in the back. I sit and write to your grave cen-
ter. There's no mysterious thing. The particles that
connected you came and went. We use heavier and
heavier words and no map. Only falling avails us. This
is some beginning, a frag of freak dream. All things in
line, stable, like some pitch you made when we ex-
isted. I'm out of coffee and my veins don't throb. I'm
just sweet, checking the grey plastic in all the aisles
of our dumb civilization. In every shack a computer,
belittled lamb of sod. I write this thing damned near
every day. Voices and music overlay. By whatever is
useless, we tug the snow down. Trouble is for beauty
and the dead.

Marshes Under Mannahatta

Secretly, like fire. Apartments touch a bang touch in nineteen something nine. All shining wood grain is covered with rusted hasps and squares. Names in the ceiling own their leaving faces. Antic ghosts stay lonely in your dream each night, until you make a sea to drown. They are satisfied and leap and gulp air with anti-joy, sleeping for collision. Frantic cities gather your ocean, build sky arms and tangle your lungs. Everything that was above is under. Surprised faces glint in little mirrors falling from pockets and purses. People see that they themselves are mere image. Saws and hands warble, nothing. Nothing when you look at the time. Nothing when the bridges are lit with sailors' fire.

You.

You will collect many many lives. & you will live them all. & you will wear out many pants. & skirts & shirts & minds. & you will one day find yourself lost in a wood. & you will laugh about this strange wood, with its wildly bent trees, curling branches which bear no resemblance to your home trees. Even their leaves will be refreshing to look at. & you will sleep in the beds of weird people, wondering what they wonder about, how they see the world, where their minds' eyes go, what doctrines they have renounced. Imagine how many times you will see yourself, and in what mirrors! Watching your face change & change.

& you will sleep many nights listening to the sound of a train. Many trains, planes & deserts without end. & sometime you might find yourself stuck without a car, or money, or phone. Perhaps by a roadside. Perhaps on a far pristine beach. Or on the deck of a ship, at sea for days. You will reflect on the magic of all you have seen, all you have yet to see, all you have yet to know. You will wear out many thoughts, rely on many friends, read the treatises of many night skies, & glittering stories in the pavement of many cities.

You will smile at the faces of children whose languages you cannot understand, in parks & on streets with signs you cannot read. You will love & leave countless jobs, pour your whole soul into great, shaping causes. & you will meet the ghosts of people who made you who you are. Or—perhaps more accurately—you will visit the ghosts of your oncenesses. Then, again, you will find incongruent objects & instruments in the drawers & houses of new friends & new lovers, hold them to your ear or eye & listen to their new music, however dissonant. Your youth will last a very long time. You will marvel at the mystery of new lovers' bodies, & the mystery of your own body made new. This is all as it should be.

You will taste the fruits of a hundred countries, distilled into a hundred liquors. They will warm you. You will wonder about your ghosts: Who have they become? & what wor(l)ds? At times, all of this will feel as if you are grasping after air, or after a morning mist. At times it will feel like you know something. Something true & concrete.

You will know things. Over & over you will make yourself new, feel the new shiver of a new love, a new range, someone you can learn with. All of this is an again-&-again thing. The landing lights of a thousand airports. The distinct smell of a thousand rains. Meals of a million worlds. Moments of cold stillness & the fear of death. & moments of ecstatic whirling light. Desires met, or perhaps not. Wishes made & unmade.

Decade after decade you will extend your hand or open your arms to worried friends. They will do the same. Again & again you will do this. & frequently, one ghost in particular will also think on you. Over & over you will both wonder. Your pasts will be a blur, a mosaic, a retinue of haunted groves, & a tessellation of crowded selves. Dance your present & your séance. & I will dance mine. & what then?

For Them

Am I nowhere then, now that she's forgotten how we touched?

Fuck. It was something like love. And I couldn't pick it up. But every book has to have a last word. Even if it's not real.

And maybe there is someone like me, living just a few years ahead or behind, who knows all that I know, and one thing more: that lost things can be regained. That yesterday will come around again. That the end is only the abridged version.

Regarding Pain

Sometimes the thing I try to do is feel all my pain at exactly the same time. The pain in my legs from running too hard, the pain in my chest from my lonely pleasure, the pain in my back from my bicycle crash, the pain in my temple because I don't see my grandma enough, the pain in my left knee from when I carried Butch on my shoulders and stepped into a ditch, the pain in my cheeks and stomach from one recent and particularly premature goodbye, the pain in my eyes from the time I saw what I shouldn't have seen (a death too young). I think of all this and I try to bring all this physical pain right up to the surface, all at the same time: the itch, the heat, the dull knot, the ache, the pressure, the stab...I let them all take me over, fill me up, so there isn't any idea of me left that isn't pain. Pain haha pain haha.

And then he just spins there, a pain man, a hot popcorn kernel whizzing around in a kettle about to pop... but he doesn't pop...he just spins and spins, getting hotter and hotter and the walls of his skin begin to turn black and smoke...and still he gets hotter... and a little orange flame forms and dances across his surface and his face cracks and falls away and his eyes light up, sending Fourth of July sparks everywhere and the full moon begins to wobble in its orbit around the earth from the incredible nuclear heat of this man made of pain spinning faster than a quark, faster than Einstein ever dreamed. A new and very unstable source of gravity forms and drags all sorts of unknown elements out of the center of the earth's molten core and they blast upwards towards the moon, which has begun to rumble and tremble. And weird milky stuff the color of Brie oozes out of the cracks in the moon's surface. And all the people of planet Earth are out of their beds now (half of them were awake already anyway) and they look up into the sky or down at the fissures forming in the rupturing earth and they begin to feel all their pain too, because of a strange chemical associative effect from the scorching speed and intensity of the man made of pain going round and round haha haha.

And before anybody knows what to do or how to do it the whole shitshow makes a sound like the puff of air from the device the eye doctor uses to shoot in your pupil during your eye exam and it all disappears. And then...Nothing. Just a faint smell of unpopped popcorn and a vast and endless space. And Werner Herzog in a space capsule with a hand-held camera over his shoulder pointing into the blackness saying to himself: "Yesss. Yesss. Haha. Yesss. I knew it. Thiss wass the right time."

ii.

My gracious silence, hail!

—Coriolanus

On Myth

I can't come at it from silence because ownership is myth, property is myth, borders are myth. As is body. We believe body harder than the others, but it's myth without reason, despite organization. To come at it from silence would be to see clearly from inside a clear room, devoid of air, color, or touch. To see clearly from silence is to move in a river, sit as a storm, wait as a mountain. No borders, no property. No myth but wind, laughing in your morning hands.

Small Things

Small things get smaller. The life lived is for choosey choosers. This won't get used, so I can reveal secrets here. Once I imagined me a girl; I did me up in brambles and berries and stalked a rooftop, colluding with voices pointed outward. I relished the stomping sound of rain and being a slanting body on a rolling day. I chose time for my thoughts to wander in. I shucked music, shucked prayers, shucked being elusive, gave myself wholly to my new gown, woven of cakes and trains. I felt good in my gown, walked without stumbling, awed myself silly. The rain was good to feel on my hands, on my rippled skin. I looked up the hill and saw the outline of the steps I would take. I took them. I felt I could fit into any bottle, any shell. Even sand was known to me. It was a dream or something. I thought I was rusting and that was all right. Someone was sighing out of my mouth, using my voice to get away.

The Auroch And The E

Upon moving into my new apartment I discovered under the floorboards the remains of a perfectly preserved auroch, which had died suddenly but not violently, some forty thousand years ago. It still had its pair of piercing horns and a musky leather smell emanating from its impressive hide. I ran my hand across the body, marveling at what was once a great musculature, the kind that inspired earlier persons to paint its likeness upon the walls of their caves, in and out of trance. I found myself riveted by the large gaping holes where its eyes had been, and the hooves seemed as if they had just come from some magnificent thundering plain, bits of rock and ancient brown moss clung to the shaggy hair at the end of the forelegs.

I felt that the correct and most effective way to do this marvel justice would be to turn it into a piano-forte or harpsichord and invite all my old friends and lovers to come and appreciate this beast as well as my own appetite for curiosity and endless innovation. Besides, it is not every day that you have an auroch with which to theorize over a glass of soda with fresh lime.

I began my preparations in earnest, wringing my hands daily, deliberating over whether to have the creature embalmed straightaway and then install a keyboard over the top of the form of the great animal; or, to carefully cut into its hide, open its prehistoric innards and coat the ribs with several layers of a fine shellac, and then build my instrument within its dried guts. This seemed to me a grand question: Should I enact an art that forces itself beyond the boundaries of occasion and setting, or should it complement and accompany the unfoldings of its immediate environs?

I was at an impasse.

To this end, I took particular note of the gorgeous "e" at the end of the perfectly plausible and temporarily comforting word "impasse." The letter spun endlessly through mental space, now pulsing hugely and with crackling potential at the start of a word like "erogenous," now playing a supportive role, yet not imposing its will or ineluctable identity too harshly beyond the boundaries of the scene, as in its second appearance in the word "cathected."

To be sure, I was caught in a pleasant conundrum. One sunny afternoon, after days of indoor contemplation of "e" while sitting over the carcass of my auroch, I came to a bright realization. I decided that I should, for inspiration, wedge the heel of my bare foot into the eye socket of the great auroch, and with my hands build a great "e" out of lucite and place within it a coiled string of blue Christmas lights. I did so, and upon entering homes of friends and old flames, I would plug my creation into the nearest outlet and call it the bridge between the snort and the kick.

Overseasoned

We are not supposed to salt our underwear.
Everyone knows this.
But still…
Taking it slow controls the weather.
Citizens are gathered up and bit by bit
Tossed into major and minor piles
Of gentleman road dust.

Some constructions are paper,
Some fancy sand.
Some ask a person to hold on
Way too long.

We both have haloes now
From all the brutality
And waiting.

But I must have you know,
In poems and in weather:
My -ness is heavily you.

Your Own Spring

This is the article without phrase. Then the going gets away from us. I'm to familiarize myself with the machine. I'm the machine. You watch the way the water bends. You bend water and live from a long way away. You stand in a pile. You collect, gather, and grade. Your hair is the hair of the earth, the reason for dreaming, the smashing tulip of a trajectory foretold. These eagles, these talons, these scallions smell like spring essence; it's always more another way around. Then you ride by the path where you are the journey, the child, the instant of lines on a window. Someone looks out at you with a hand waving. You notice skin, and wonder in collections. You visit memories as a drifter. You are a new darkness made whole by the secrets you enjoy. Yes, you enjoy them, they make you. They represent your own skin, as it folds over you, in vegetal coolness. Think of children, of being a child. Your work takes you very far away.

The Beast That Lunges

The best thing about remembering is that it's in your hands. You revolt against sleep and become a phantom in time, moving through rooms and visions as a wiry, feral child. You don't need words to eat, to find shelter. You taste water in air and move to it with your thirst. You kneel over a lake at night. The outline of your face is a surprise. You breathe hard and lunge into recollection. You run backwards and laugh at your heelprints in the earth. Snakes slide back to their skins. Fires grow into trees. Pearls soften to sand. You unwrite the future for the happy beast you are becoming. Rain whispers quietly upward. The past begins to show. Clarity is dimness. Your hands as clouds, as fins, as roaming notes.

His Language Of Need

And he makes them, and makes them, and he makes
animal sounds, makes animal sounds and the day
is, and the day he makes animals sounds the day
runs into ruin, as the sounds run and he makes it, he
makes them run, he rolls them, rubs the river, the day
changes, he makes the day's changes and it makes
him, it names him, the animals name him, they go to
him, he seeks them, they turn to him and he turns the
day, the day runs with him, makes him something,
goes toward rivers, makes changes.

His sounds make changes, make them bread, make
them with eyes and long uninterrupted swing sets
with horns where eyes are, horns above lightning,
feelings in the deep, in the war, he makes war with
animals in his mind, the animals don't befriend him
if he makes war, and he makes it, he puts his face
aside, he runs with the combinations, he retools
things, makes everything run in the belly of animals,
of scared people he knows, of walls, and he resigns.
He goes to the basement, he keeps his tools there,
he makes sounds there, makes words and elephants,
big elephant words that carry him in his war with
words and animals and walls and the frayed ends of
his liver that he wonders about in his meditations, he

sweeps aside things with his hands, his hands roll the grass up and take everyone to the river and to the train tracks and to the prison cell.

He shadows his hearing under snakes, he envelopes crying, his tears tear his jaw down, he slumps, he feels horror, he goes to the people, they cry around him, they take his liver out, he looks at it, they are afraid, he is afraid, they feed him to animals and his liver regrows him, he is alive again, he is not angry with people, they took care of him, they did what was necessary, they eliminated the ardor, they followed through, they made him whole again, they fed him, they gave him a sen1se of when the time would be right for him to go on a journey, he went, he came back, they received him.

Everyone was having lunch, they sat him down, he told his story, they ate his story while they listened to him speak, there were bones making noises in the rooms inside their houses, the war was in their houses and the man told them of their war and they ate lunch, they had lunch next to the man, gave him sandwiches and salads and soups and they saw something of a feeling coming out of him and he was alone in that he could not feel them seeing that something was happening to him, he was alone and they were together and they felt him give way, he felt himself give way, there was something to say and he couldn't say it, they listened and he said it but they could only hear their own hearing.

Them feelings, they thought, them feelings he's having, it's the war, they thought, it's the war, and they asked if he wanted to leave them and he said no, and they stopped eating and asked him to sit down again and he took his arms and did something with his arms, used them in a way they could not understand, he made new words, made words without sounds or symbols of sounds, made unconnected wheelings of arm words and he left them thinking he might come back again, then the sky allowed for his passing, the light covered his shoulders in orange and he was washed clean of even his name and feelings and any other forms he used when he was alone, now he was his own together with the dawn and the rich animal sounds coming from the river and his newly formed words, that only he could understand.

He Tangerines Your Crow's Feet

i.

He wallops a few flim-flammers on his way to break-
fast. Chlorine eyes and a shank of ice function as a pen.
He knows his target, trusts his team, stirs ellipses into
the mix. Frogmen gather at the corners of his mouth.

He brandishes a cutlass. His cordage is wavy in a nau-
tical light. He sees the microchip in your wobbly hand,
notices you're fine, memory's fine, nostalgia's fine. He
keeps force out of the equation this time, and knocks.

Heavy in window trousers, he ossifies your weedy
arms. Beering around in the old dark: negative ray,
positive horn.

ii.

Music is grout in the spaces between you. He rues
time, bumbles lines before a Naga King, rearranges
green curry molecules, feels the sting of an old sea
tune, "as hit is breued in þe best boke of romaunce."
Amid an earthy clangor, "bronze by gold," he "hear[s]
the hoofirons steelyringing." He is goatman, dogbeard,
beewolf, stunned electric wire, a wintry field resonance.

His hair and nails keep growing, looking for a sandwich. He is Karate.

He parties with one ear open, listens to your baby blue hair. His arms go down into the earth and his neck flops thisaway on the pavement. You see him spin, giddily, in a fly eye.

iii.

He toils in sand with an old radio, bings out to roll-
er music. He wakes to clacking trains. People get
up every day and look down at the earth. Fields of
muscle sweat out strength, and asphalt needs cars
to stay viable, pliable. Holidays abound like so many
founders of thought. Thus, he records his celebration.

He pockmarked the sun today, used a stain instead of
a hose, ate seeds of true rain. He'll toe the hammer,
tundra down your knees. Is there a dog you scatter
windward, enough to make it back to burnt lands, hover
and run in blue mercy? Then go. His field awaits. He's
all sorts of there. Merely, merely, life can only seem.

He paints a cat on your nunchucks, blazes on your bike
wheel. Why go rambling when you have mind waves
to walk on? And you do walk, year after fall, down again
in a storm of baying dogs. Roll to see if you survive a
fight with a giant man, or a world without chance.

iv.

He is in the middle. Weeds gloss stone. Kids mean-
der in a remembering place. Fire for a stove opens a
gate. This is ancient purpose or animals. Living in vast
thought wakes the eating mind this day; forgiveness
postures up the road and sheds light, guilt, and every
sick. Together you become an old lizard.

He reads uncharted books, maps your quest: a séance. He gets you all the way to a knowing country, maybe India. Horses in the clean streets, washing fish in handy rain, yellow carvings. All carpenters wander in search of inspiration, end in trees. He looks to the end, an origami man.

What Are Your Crashing Into?

What are you crashing into? I'm crashing into my hands, my beard, and my strange society. Lately my hands are too much a human boy, trying to pull ideas out of rock. I'll tell you what I really wish. I wish my left hand was a guitar and my right hand knew how to play. Just my hand, though, I don't want my mind in the mix, mucking everything up. You know how that always happens. I say to my life, "I'd sure appreciate a little love, or a sunset, or a steak done just right." And it gives me those things. But whenever I ask it to give me what's really missing, what would fill the cavern inside me, what would turn me into a real song instead of just a little rattle in the breeze, life gives me some birthday cake and a few lines about how little time is left. In those hidden night moments when I can touch loss itself, my breastbone is a string pulled tight enough to pop. My heart underneath is a hollering shade, like those thirsty ghosts Odysseus meets, who crowd in when they smell the scent of blood. To drink makes them feel real for a moment. At night my eyes grow red with tears for all the people I don't know, all the thoughts I have to keep pickling in my head. I can't tell the world I'd like to be as wind, coursing over mountainsides and into cities, through all your houses and rooms, touching everything, touching everyone, touching all of you.

Child Moon Crowns A Shirt

Then stay not a brain fever. Instead shirk old wonder in monk cars in clone real must, must mustard. Driven by not night, waiting back until youth bereft and sorted goes swaying. Child moon crowns a shirt. It's all very sane as we planned a last weekend in hell, over Europe, over dangerous skies, over leaning into water. Never been on a boat together, as a function of being American. Sways at docksides, beaches in last gleam, shows in holy studios. Hardwood floors where dumb friends play cards and vibrations.

Variation On A Meme By Andrew Marvell

Light from the first city,

the tea garden,

like grass under clouds,

is predictable.

What happens is not.

How the New Year moves,

what it swings toward,

or away from,

is everybody's guess.

With tides,

with fog,

with a movement of hands

and shouting down cans

on long strings,

I call you in words.

Each hearer hears

her own hearing,

but perhaps a bit more.

This year is drawing to its close,

and cold rains beckon.

Let us find an umbrella,

walk long on the sand,

and see what transpires

under willing soles.

He Is Very Good

For the hell of it, you go and come back, take dictation from an advanced being, and go to the bathroom with a house on your shoulders. It's heavy, and your Spain won't budge. You lift everything you see in search of more, and instead you find less. There are little Japanese figurines in the corners, laughing with your eyes. You get all the varieties, every week. The Bob Dylan isn't shy, he's adorable. The stance is wide, the girls are everywhere, white sheets and The God-damned Sound and the Fury. My mother was a fish. He likes sex, you can tell. She's out here. He's watching Diego. She's writing. He's William Carlos Williams and Cubist painting. She's writing. She's dealing with a pain in her neck. She never tells where it hurts and keeps her bullet safe inside. Good morning. The humiliations have been spectacular. She kissed him in the middle of dinner, in the middle of Geography. He's having no luck with the ladies. He's capital, just capital. He's catching up. He finds New York brief, another round, misses doing things you wouldn't expect. Cheers to our noble profession. He drinks, for the first time in a long time. He does business in Europe. He didn't know it was for sale. His wife's lawyer won't leave him a pot to think. Excuse us. He would very much like some wine. He drinks a martini with an onion in it. She doesn't know why she picks the wrong boys. She wonders what is wrong with her. She's got the wrong style. He'll fix her. She looks at him. He is very good. Yes, yes, it's okay, it's good. They are in the pool. He assumes they are all well-off. He should take up a hobby. He's smarter than he's ever been in his life, and his brain is more agile. His muscles are remembering their skills. Her father will take care of you, he likes having you around. You're beautiful and you don't take too much. You're not possessive. You can be with anyone you want. As you can see we're very tired. You don't want to sleep. He gave away our room. She's twenty one. Her father makes love at the other end of the pool. He gives her a bottle of gin. There are riots in the street. California was spectacular. The people were what was okay with it. He eats mints to mask the scent of gin. He's making it rain. He's opening her kimono. He's surrounded by white linens.

That Can-Do Spirit

> *"The universe is time travel."*
> —Lisa Cooper

Miguel de Unamuno was wrong ➔ it's not our own reflection we fall in love with when we look in our lover's eyes ➔ it's the air of our own breath bounced back at us by the breath of that other breather. In this way you always take away my out-breath when you leave. And I can control my muscles and make my heart go 185 beats per minute ➔ but I cannot make a text turn into life ➔ magic *is* the imagination, we know it, we face it ➔ And if you think about the muscles and the bones in your face as you smile, you will be too anatomically aware to be truly smiling, and your smile will be an act of musculature, only the ghostly trace of your emotion. ➔ So being aware of emotion is always only noticing its after-effects. O, thought itself is an apocalypse, which is just okay as a broken-but-adequate way to navigate anyone's life ➔ So every poem for the next 1000 years will be about my dream of you, and in every life after this life when we meet I will already be writing about you, and neither of us will know it, and as we fall and fuck and leave each other over and over I will dream this dream, somewhere deep and far away from memory, and reinforce the pattern, again and again. But 1000 years from now I will be finished, no matter what we have become to each other → and I will take a deep breath and open my metaphysical wings and dissolve into air and be done with dreaming → and if by then my air car has a faulty engine, I will become all air car, or an economist. And, of course, Miguel de Unamuno wasn't always wrong. And I dream about you every night.

Tender Wolfman

Barnacles and the fright they elicit: hardly an issue in real time. Hiking and hiking. The journalistic tendency to document this thought. This time, when we ascend the mountain there will be cake, made by a future us that travelled there to support our struggling past. Rotors, fanblades, the gaze of an infant, all have a way of reminding. You and me and the undergrowth gather in untended places: radical distraction. Some wolfman I am, tending the most tender flower, yellow petals trembling in light wind.

A Visit From My Familiar

Tricks depend on trick thinking, on dash to sea, and cry of dogs at night. One is for writing, two is for filling wants. Light cracks through cracks in the curtains. My hand rises off this bed of its own accord, and floats above your face while you sleep. It sends warmth from my palm into your cheek. I hear sentences in my head and make movements towards you, my legs planted. I am the tree that waits for you to climb. There is thirst enough between us to dry a town. I see you at your desk, writing and wanting. Sometimes you cry in your longing and I send my ghost brain to your fingers and eyes, that they might be touched. Lamps above you flicker and curtains shift. You breathe hard as my face and arms appear. My hands move over you in slow and heavy sweeps. You feel them as you write, your desk an urgent shelf of stories. Your sentences well and burst. My beard on the back of your neck makes you shiver and smile.

The Storms

The storms have thrashed these houses, these streets. It is winter and yet feels like flowers from what we say. The snow is in my head already. But your words are deciding things. We have said sleep and lying down and other things like how the world might go. The passage over mountains has made things. We have turned and seen each other looking. I like that you look for me, and I like to look for you. I taste orange in my mouth after a wish. It does the opposite of sting. We might look at the numbers on my door as we walk out. Stucco grey cloud heads roll in to see our earth arms. It will keep happening, this hat of desire. It will happen and keep relocating in our limbs, the recollections, laughter between us. Not the ones that got away but the ones that got to go, we'll find far and foreign flavors and bring them back. As the dust that fills the world makes it old and new and clay each day, so will I make you.

Coughing Winter

So instead I have to feel.

I brought the poem a ball,

Coughed out winter,

Balled the poem effectively,

Ate sausage and pepper,

And remembered your shoes.

All of them were just so-so,

But I didn't think.

Watching the lauded poet

Listen to the grand famous poet

I'm glad I ride a bicycle,

Glad I know how to fight

With my hands and legs,

And how to use a machete.

Today's a dad's birthday:

My dad, mine twice.

Keeping my head shaved

Keeps me closer to the word.

I'm faint everywhere but the bed.

I'm a DaVinci of the bed (please don't believe me).

And DaVinci wrote upside-down and backwards

Because he *tried*.

He tried a lot of tangled light.

I took you on my subway.

You moved away from my _____.

I chose to be a frogman going into you,
And still you are the you of my poems,
Even as I try,
Backwards and upside-down.

Mini Sunset

How about a micro twilight, right after lunch? We'll meet before the day goes back to grinding, before all the real work needs to get back to itself. We can sneak into a supply closet, turn out the lights, think some bending thoughts. We'll write stuff that's free of the institution in our heads. The world hears us listening all the time anyway; shouldn't we make the most of it? The pants I put on are almost falling off, I'm always nibbling on seaweed, and I'm beginning to hear fish think, in my little apartment by the sea. In our tiny dusk we won't make any plans, we'll just crawl into a big sundress together and laugh at the glowing stars I stuck to my ceiling. And music? Yeah, big guitar sounds like swans, blue riffs that guarantee a decent hermetic seal.

Take It All Off

Stash the robot in a major drawer. Stand alone in the rain cabin. Find a human in your mumble. This is to be shown, to be exploited in the first place you find. You shave your face free of your body, point at the moon, find a way to crow. Look at the signature across the cold hand, the knee that answers. It's downright lyrical, this hallowed humane coat. Both of us nattered and palsied. Hey, you know how we used to go up on the roof and get down to our underwear and fancy ourselves important? Yeah, the fish tank has only gotten smaller.

Induction into the Society of Epic Wanderers: Cancelled due to non-attendance. We got high marks in vision, mysticism, high school. We fancied and felt admired. Something came down from a cave. A figurine and a bat had a message: Watch your tender head. Nobody talks like this, seriously. Except this freaking page.

Textually, there are no seasons. Only Summer and Winter, Sandwich and Fall.

The Hat Of The World

What is the pantry and what the relic, what the groundsman and what the fuse, what the fidgeter and what the quay? The pants, sheets, and the queasy feeling and the trying after glory and dancing, and the apartments and the staying and the leaving. The it, the identification of it, the shine and sadness and lightning and stability of children and stomach. And seeing the them, the endless them, the fleeing and returning and going and simple happiness of making words and going with ease. The non-tooth-pulling aspect of freedom from fear and staying in that bubble. In Tahiti, in ease in Tahiti. In finding, we get happily lost in oceanic striving, letting go and getting lucky. It all happens away from us, close. We seek to sit in a silence that golds us up. And we do. That silence golds us and we shatter the rain-frame and run through, collide with the pervasive sand in our shoes. Our eye-corners, our happy peopled skin, brown in the sun. Sharing it all without wanting or waiting, just sitting in the gold of silence, the hat of the world.

The Thinnest Thread

Burnt and burning and the return of hows that heap the fire. Yellow leaves do the candle thing. This is not that. This is not the papier-mâché world we clotted up and rolled, our arms dirty and sand in cracks. This heaven thing: memory of a blue song in the hollow of an attic guitar. You play for me, I gather my belongings, sit and listen. The world is all alive with little Shinto creatures, humming in corners, everywhere softening. I have tea, we look at the designs on your arm, the meat is served and it is all very grand. The thinnest thread is all I need.

Bulk Rate

Happy this, happy that, happy your listing mariner's feet busting a Monday window. Egg baby charcoal baby igneous baby gone. Rough cut ice cream, tumble down bastards at the wall ate free. This king, this emperor, childless guru with rustic charms and sibilant coordination, his shanty shoes and tundra pals went down. From storm eye fragrant leaves, from shadows and bulk rate images dart circles and concert memories. Throats have worlds. Casting about for sheep eyes, our dice hands find a bier of burning nights, naked in water and wind. Grow cold, grow without mercy, grow 'til globe gets along.

Field X

—after Rene Garcia, Jr.'s painting "X Wing"

Did you see me when I looked? Did your sparking hands split for words, come down in a hot wheel fall? Risen and running in hills and edges I stood and cranked my arms back, wondering hard. You broke every border, all things held, and every born thing. Even air felt a roar of fire, pulse and crumble of weird empires, love burning into paint. Watch land, watch raking movements, watch open heads and stolen safety. I, as vagabond, teeter "omnitropically (the in in the which of who where what wells)," roll my mat out, bow down, crooked arrow of a minion, of a man. Out of the screens of story, all that glitters might be ghost; I sleep alone or in pairs to find out. Do you hear them, galaxies of this able flower, earning wind? Among sprays of wild lupine will you find me in The Force?

On My Burial Mound

Yes. To go down and not find relics is hardly a future. For me. For you. What is this refraction? What is this change? What heart in me spools outward now? How is it the you I write to is both you and me? I am trying not to build emotion, I am trying to hoist story to the level of poem and smash it through a sweet reflector. As for my hands, they find things to do with you. Buoyant, they feel strong when I grin and strong when I fall. This upward gust is not a thief of seclusion, but close. Imagine. Some nothing dashes through you and you fear no memory. Instead you sit. You sit in the memory of nothing and you bellow ever stronger. It's the fate of every search, every forking light. You distant shimmer, you weed, you you. Something is home when you say it is. Words make things home, not this scattered mass of hoods and quiet. Nowhere has me; I stand atop my burial mound. I look down and in. I will take you to my ancestors, to my tectonic beginnings, to me before I knew words.

On Previous Days

You, that book, that ruggedized case, lost on logic. You took your meanings down, along with your pea-coat, your savvy beatitudes, your empirical globe. You caught fish, showed the kids "how it's done." You weren't prideful or too teacherly. You just wandered into the scene of the moment and gathered necessities. Sure, bodies decomposed under the floor and wraiths howled in dark corners. You were aware of them all, but you played life focused, also not denying librettos, spinning hubcaps, beach days. A man was responsible, then gone. In the middle of it a feeling of fellowship, rivers going by, rock formations in the sun, boots going up some mountains. Your own feet stepped behind you on previous days.

Uniform Din Horizon Murk Unending Absence Equation For Planets And Medicine Illness Of Drain And Loss

My dirty dog dark I need water I need stark I need my cold head full this letter for lusting and freezing new ear for seeing and this open window a raw gaunt shield of bracken body for taking down flumes of old hell and torn baggies of light and chambers of brushing sublimated trains aghast with wormflies hastening and broadening to fill yon voided bed oh mimics with candy oh breach of imperfect trust and secret world sans atom or atmosphere collude with igneous houses gathered in emptiness I flank and cranes wreck the yellow dress relay quiet moats forward of winter bastions earthy black ponds of bursting metonymy.

Here

Here's what you remember: You remember the rain, and going into the rain. You remember trees giving way to ashes and ashes giving way to hands. And you wished for a galaxy of grey panels, of water coming down in cloaks, of melted nights blending together on trains, near lakes, in puddles and fields of blackbirds. You gathered up your sheets, moved with the movement of air through a window, placed your hands against cool glass. You preferred everything, in general, and you spoke always about flowers and young mourners and celebrations with fire. In every word you spoke, you heard the echo of water. It began as memory and became a drumming of white petals against a wet roof. Animals forgot themselves and you twisted into their happy movements. The pink angles of day returned and you wore a flower to commemorate everything.

I'll Memory You

The grey granite of big intentions has me in a worldly crunch. Wobbling in time before time, we saw each other and ran towards life. What innocence is it that I see inside my own head and watch microscopic sharks thrusting everywhere without pretense? What rain and what kaleidoscope? Put your hand in mine and we can sleep until the end of sleep. And small fingers come through autumn. A little garden ripple and then quiet. No one moving, and no one going to move. The them that we call us wavers and embraces—lost needles finding their way to beats. And crumpled creatures, breathing tiny yawns of singed relief. No one gazed the way we gazed that way, that day. All was a subcutaneous tide of sighs. Water in me and me missing my cave. It's too long a way to because. Because you found a way to think the emblems out of dust. I was wrong and right, the way a ship eventually goes down. Someone knows they should sing a song, and everyone pretends to listen.

Sleeping Hot

It's not about infatuation, it's about how you dream and how I want to learn even that. The way you roll slowly from side to side while you're falling makes me want to touch your leg. The night is long and cool and I am awake, watching you in the minimal blue. Another little breather breathing into the dark. You might have held onto that last thought for a while, but I saw it leave you when your hands opened. I put my hand on the back of your knee and you grumble, then fall back into the well. I let you drift and feel the depth of our bed, watch the rows and rows of days we'll spend together unfold out to the horizon. I gather them around me, bigger and warmer than any blanket.

Acknowledgements

Genuine gratitude to the editors of the publications in which the following poems first appeared:

"Regarding Pain": *Manawaker Studios Flash Fiction Podcast* (2019).

"Staying," "Them Just Goes": *Fact-Simile* 12 (2019).

"The Bath Of Time": *Green Linden* (2016).

"The Beast That Lunges": *Word Fountain* (2016).

"A Peculiar Caravan": *The Tishman Review* (2016).

"Take It All Off," "The Auroch And The E," "Traveling Outside": *Esque* 2 (2011).

"A Cork in the Floor Comes Out," "Beating Due Headfakes": *Eoagh* 6 (2011).

"I Haven't Been Comfortable Enough To Take Anyone For Granted In Years": *Shampoo* 37 (Spring 2010).

Special thanks to Kristallia Sakelariou for helping to locate Arturo Elizondo, who painted "Young Kafka, a Dalai Lama."

Very special thanks also to Tenney Nathanson for asking, again and again, about The Ten Thousand Things.

Matthew Rotando is a Fulbright Fellow and holds degrees from Duke University (BA), Brooklyn College (MFA), and the University of Arizona (MA, PhD). He is professor of English Literature and Creative Writing at SUNY Nassau Community College. He bicycles regularly with Dickinson, Borges, and Neruda.